W0246956

The GUCCI STYLE PRINCIPLES

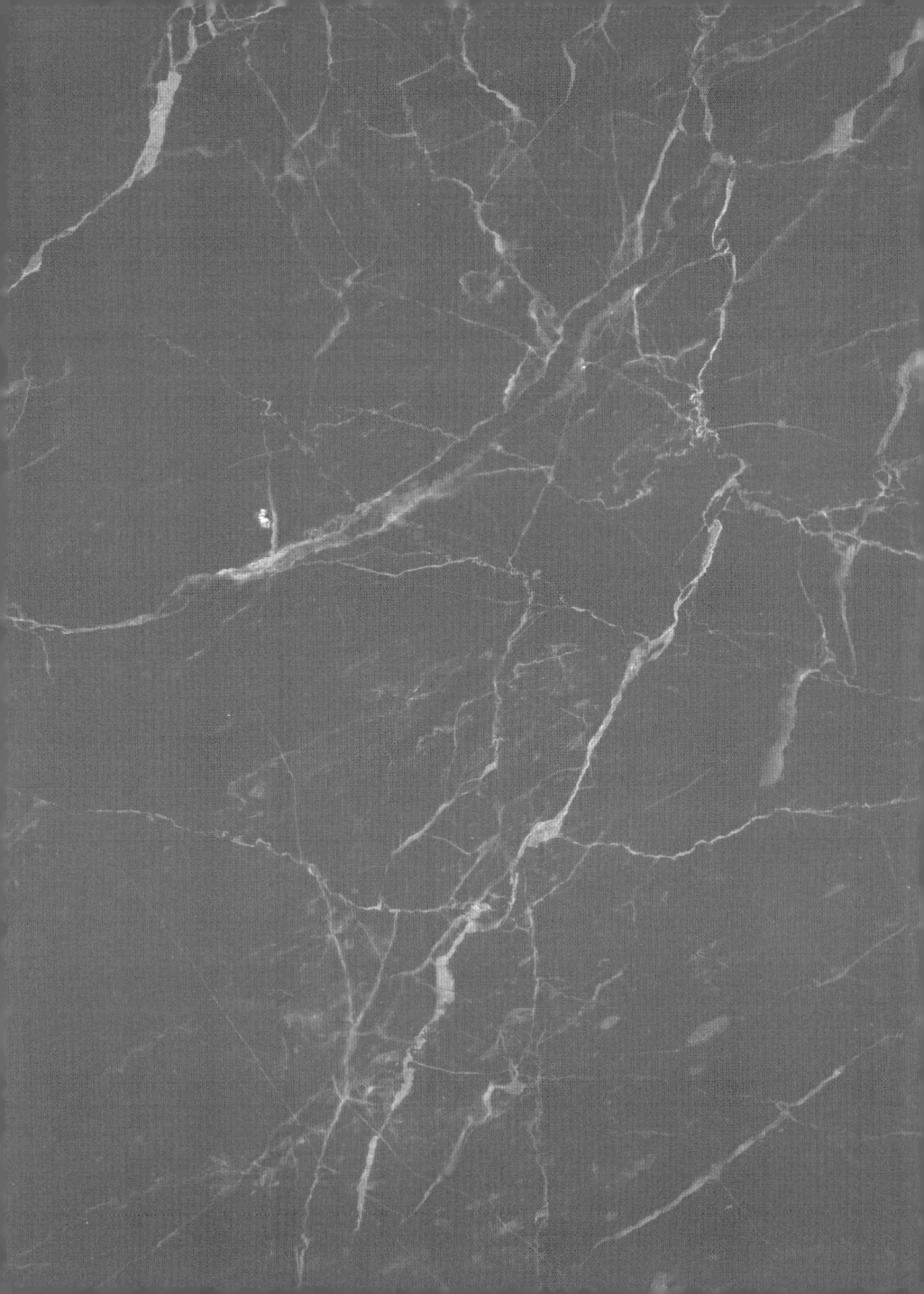

The GUCCI STYLE PRINCIPLES

BE INSPIRED, TRANSFORM HOW YOU DRESS

HANNAH ROGERS

Unofficial and unauthorised

EBURY
PRESS

Intro

duction

Gucci.

It's the Italian label that was started by a hotel bellboy, with a global reach and vast influence. So, chances are that you've heard of Gucci – but do you think you know everything about it? It is the twisting backstory, cast of key characters and scene-stealing fashion that we are going to explore in this book.

There is a lot of ground to cover. Gucci was founded over a century ago. Since, it has grown from a boutique Florentine luggage brand to fully fledged luxury giant. Its logo is recognised the world over as an indicator not just of what is tasteful, but also what is cool. You'd be hard pushed to find a celebrity who hasn't worn it at least once; ditto a metropolitan city without a Gucci boutique.

It has transformed from a family-run business to a jewel in the crown of the designer conglomerate Kering. It has also been a home to some of fashion's greatest creators. Tom Ford worked at Gucci; so did Alessandro Michele. As for the Guccis themselves, they used the brand as a battleground for salacious in-fighting – all of which has made for quite addictive source material.

Make no mistake: Gucci is a universe of pure, unadulterated and high-voltage glamour, which is why so many of us want a bit of it in our wardrobes. But instead, how about letting it gently influence your outfits every day? Each chapter of the following pages focuses on particular Gucci items, eras and aesthetics, with the aim of distilling its core style principles.

I hope you can use them when mixing your own style cocktail.

So, whether you want to find the perfect pair of loafers, consider yourself more 'Ford fabulous' than 'Michele mad' or simply want to know how to bring a bit of glamour to your beauty routine, let this book be your guide to getting the ultimate Gucci look.

The origins of Gucci

It looks Italian; it sounds – when pronounced correctly ('G-oo-chi' not 'G-uck-y', in the avoidance of any doubt) – Italian and, as the signature red and green stripes that come on its stylish wares indicate, it is, in its very DNA, Italian. So, you probably think Gucci's story begins in Milan, perhaps even Rome. Actually, no.

It is not the Tuscan capital of Florence, either. Gucci did open its first boutique there, and the man who founded the brand was a Florentine, too. But the spot where he came up with the idea for his future power brand was miles away from his native hub of Renaissance art and architecture. Technically, the Gucci brand was conceived in London.

Surprised? It is far from the most intriguing fact you'll learn in *The Gucci Style Principles*. Historic fashion houses often have juicy, prolific back stories, but Gucci's is truly rich: riddled with scandal, family in-fighting – and even a murder. Believe me when I tell you that it's got more unctuous layers than a tiramisu. (It is just as delicious, too.)

I doubt that founder Guccio Gucci (that name!) thought that his fledgling label would amount to all that. Nor that, over a century after he opened a bricks and mortar store

Left to right: Roberto Gucci, Giorgio Gucci, an unnamed associate and Maurizio Gucci outside a Gucci boutique in Paris, September 1983

with his name over the doors, there would be hundreds of outposts thriving across the globe. At the end of the nineteenth century, he was only just coming into the knowledge that there was a market for beautiful, good-quality, high-end luggage: the products Gucci was originally built on. Then, he was busy carting it around for other people, as a bellboy at one of London's most prestigious hotels, The Savoy.

This is the position he had found employment in after fleeing Florence. Keen to get away from his family's failing straw-hat business – and its subsequent bankruptcy – as a teenager, Gucci worked his way to England via freight train. A man of few means, he proved he didn't lack any ambition when he got himself on the payroll at London's iconic luxury hotel. There, he spent his days ferrying trunks, suitcases, trinkets and hat boxes around for The Savoy's high-profile clientele.

The landmark property, founded in 1889, has always been impossibly glamorous. It counts Marilyn Monroe, Sophia Loren and Frank Sinatra among its illustrious former residents, to name but a few. It remains a celebrity hotspot now – and precious to Gucci. The brand has a line of luggage it created in collaboration with The Savoy and, running the riverside length of the hotel's fifth floor, is the Gucci-designed Royal Suite.

Wherever in the world you are reading this, if possible, I recommend a trip to its American Bar for a cocktail at least once in your life. You don't need to be a guest to visit it and you never know who might be sipping on a tipple in the next-door booth. It was certainly this – being surrounded by the rich and famous Savoy residents (and every one of their decadent accessories) – that gave Mr Gucci his lifetime objective: to own a luxury label of his own.

But we are just at the beginning. There were still some stops on the way to get there. After leaving The Savoy, seed for his future well planted, Gucci reportedly took a role at Wagons-Lits, a European overnight train company, with which he travelled the continent. He eventually returned to Florence four years later, where he met his wife Aida Calvelli, married her and adopted her toddler son Ugo. The pair went on to have four children, whom you will come to know well in this book – Grimalda (1902), Aldo (1905), Vasco (1907) and Rodolfo (1912). Another son, Enzo, passed away in childhood.

Florence is a city with centuries of merchant history. It is now a UNESCO World Heritage Site, originally built on beauty: both admiring it and creating it. Michelangelo was a Florentine and so were Galileo and Da Vinci. It is viewed by many as a nucleus of craftsmanship and merchandising – the perfect place, then, to build a luxury brand.

That's why Gucci was able to work at a leather firm when he first returned there. Such workshops were plentiful in Florence and, after the First World War, Gucci took a job at the Italian luggage brand Franzi – a suitable place to learn the ropes and set up for his future endeavours.

Florence's globally drawn crowd and international, high-brow repute is also why Gucci so desperately wanted to open his shop there. He felt that Florentines understood the finer things in life. Perhaps now is a good time to mention that the Tuscans have a reputation in their home country for, well, snobbery. It all adds up to why the first Gucci store ended up in an elegant Florentine neighbourhood, at a spot on the Via della Vigna Nuova, which, in 1921, had a chic footfall that Gucci hoped would step through his doors.

It wouldn't be long before the store was a destination in its own right. Gucci was popular with Florence's tourists, initially as a destination for imported, high-end, leather luggage from Tuscan, British and German manufacturers. Gucci hand-picked those pieces but soon began stocking

items of his own design too; if he couldn't find what he wanted elsewhere, he would have it made himself. He was as exacting with his own appearance as he was with his stock: it is well reported that Gucci was a man of elegance and taste, always in sharp suits and pressed shirts.

Later, Gucci opened a boutique workshop where local craftsmen made luxe leather accessories just for him. The brand's reputation among the world's wealthiest shoppers grew for its unique, equestrian specialism: Gucci made saddles and horse harnesses as well as luggage with a sporty and sleek equine influence. A second shop in Florence followed to meet demand, then outposts in Rome and Milan. At this point, luggage remained the focal part of the business. But Gucci's journey was just beginning.

upgrade your
LUGGAGE

'Quality is remembered long after price is forgotten.'

Aldo Gucci

What better style principle to start with than the one that will really take you places – literally? It pertains to how you travel, be that long distance or just down the road for the weekend. Tell me: what state is your suitcase in right now?

If it is battered, bruised or even bright pink, then bad news: a Gucci would not be caught dead with it in tow. As you've read, the brand built its name on being the last word in luxe luggage – you know now that its founder was inspired by the trunks transported around one of the ritziest hotels in the world. That's why the first law of the brand is to upgrade yours. Chic is the watchword; elegant, too.

In short, you want your travel accessories to look expensive. But they certainly do not have to be. You can get the first-class look on an economy budget – you just need to know what to buy. See the next page for my tips on travelling like a Gucci.

1

Invest in your luggage.
That is rule number one. You should only need
to buy a set every decade – maybe even longer –
so make sure that what you buy is the best quality
you can afford.

2

Go luxe on your materials and colour palette.
In Guccio Gucci's day, only leather would do for luggage – but
how realistic is that now, given the demands of a suitcase
trundling through airports from security to the arrivals belt?

Not very. At least if you're not turning left on the plane. So, I
would advise keeping leather for hand luggage, rucksacks and
duffel bags. You can opt for vegan options, obviously, if you
prefer. Canvas bags with leather trims look just as smart.

For larger, check-in luggage, get a lightweight, hard-shell trunk
– and get your Gucci-fication via the colour. Classic neutrals
such as black or beige work, as would a dark Gucci green.

3

It's in the details.
I mean it. Guccio Gucci was a master craftsman.
Perfectly sewn seams, finished corners and sleek handles
mattered. Smart gold or metal hardware
is something to seek out, too.

4

Think outside the box.

Gucci's clients' luggage is not limited to basic bags and neither does yours have to be. There is a whole world of travel accessories that can make packing and organisation easier, and now you can even buy them in sets. Consider investing in the following items for your travel arsenal: document wallet or folio; jewellery case; laptop case; technology box (for cables, chargers and plugs); camera bag; soft packing cells to neatly divvy up your wardrobe items; cosmetics bag; watch roll. It might sound like a one-way ticket to an excess baggage weight fine, but these could actually mean you are able to fit more into your case. Trust me.

5

Get matching sets.

Nothing would be more Gucci than to match your luggage pieces. Either get them from the same store or just buy them all in the same colour.

6

Get personal with a monogram.

Adding your initials to your luggage is a shortcut to sophistication. Many brands offer monogramming as a service and you'll never lose your suitcase on the conveyor belt again.

Got that? Then, all aboard! Destination: Gucci.

learn to love

THE LOAFER

'Elegance is like manners. You can't be polite only on Wednesday or Thursday. If you are elegant, you should be every day of the week.'

Aldo Gucci

J ane Birkin wore them. So did Brigitte Bardot. Brad Pitt slipped a pair on to play his iconic role as Tyler Durden in *Fight Club* and Madonna paired hers with a silk shirt buttoned below her bra and black skinny jeans to the MTV Video Music Awards in 1995. Zoë Kravitz and Alexa Chung. Hailey Bieber, Sienna Miller and Katie Holmes. They all have one thing in common and you can spot it just south of their ankles. Yes, of course it's from Gucci – so what else could it be but a pair of the label's loafers?

Look to the pavement the next time you are in a smart bit of town if you can't place this particular shoe. The almond-toe leather loafer topped with the brand's signature gold horse-bit snaffle (more on which later, but for now, know that it is a distinctively shaped mouthpiece – two circles connected by a chain-link – that forms part of horse-riding bridle) is an icon of luxury fashion. It, and versions of it, have been invading wardrobes since it was created in 1953. Fashion editors love it; royals and businessmen do too. Further proof of its cult status can be found at The Metropolitan Museum in New York, where a pair is on permanent display.

The loafer was Gucci's first accessory to take off after luggage – and with its rise came Gucci's confirmed status as a household name. It is the shoe that stepped the label into the stratosphere, style-wise; the 'It-cessory' which became a must-have in the late sixties, yet has stood the test of time. It is very much still considered cool: in 2023 the millennial pinup Paul Mescal starred in a campaign to celebrate its seventieth anniversary, wearing the shoes with jeans and T-shirts in some images and nothing but boxers, a vest and trench coat in others.

The leather slip-on wasn't the work of Guccio, the founder we met in chapter one. Gucci's loafers were tweaked and taken up by the well-heeled thanks to his eldest son, Aldo. Under his guidance, the shoe grew into the giant status it enjoys today – not coincidentally, the brand did, too.

The year of Guccio's death – in 1953, aged 72 – was the same one in which Gucci's loafer was born. It was also the year that the family's era of infighting began. Guccio's daughter, Grimalda, had been left out of any inheritance of Gucci shares by her father, who believed that Gucci men – and men alone – should run the business. Guccio passed his company entirely over to his three sons despite the fact that Grimalda had done as much shop floor work. After a failed legal bid to claim what she felt she was owed, she never had involvement in the family business again.

You'd like to think that wouldn't happen today. Sexism aside, Guccio's death marked an exciting new chapter in

An influencer in Gucci monogram loafers

the brand's history. Aldo, who had been left in charge of all major business decisions from New York while his brothers remained in Florence, had huge expansion plans for the company. He had masterminded the opening of the label's first New York store shortly before Guccio's death, and in 1960 and 1973, there followed two more.

On the city's smartest sidewalks, the Gucci name was growing in prominence. Look skyward and you'd see its name glistening above doors of the hottest addresses in retail; glance down and you would likely spot a pair of its loafers.

Gucci had been making versions of leather moccasins since the 1930s, but until the mid-1960s the item was considered tertiary to its luggage offering. It was reportedly in the early 1950s that the men's loafer, Model 175, was designed – supposedly at the suggestion of a Gucci factory worker who had family ties to shoemaking. The price then was indicative of the item's importance to the business. You'd pay nearly 60 times the original cost for a pair now.

The original women's version came later, but it was considered ugly and quite bizarre to shoppers when it first launched in the New York store. No wonder: this was the era of the stiletto. Fashionable types could not conceive of stepping out anywhere fancy in a flat shoe.

While initially the brand could barely shift its stock, over time, the style caught on. Tides often turn in fashion and this was one of those moments: soon every savvy, sartorially minded woman wanted a pair. They saw that the slip-ons were comfortable and affordable and, most importantly, worked with several outfits.

The loafer design as we know it now came into being in 1968. The Model 360 – a slightly modified version of its predecessor, the Model 350 – became a hit. It came in every type of exotic leather (lizard, ostrich and alligator, to name a few) and several different colours. Per Sara Gay Forden's book *The House of Gucci*, the brand was selling 84,000 pairs a year in America in 1969 – and 24,000 of those were being purchased in New York.

The shoe was a sensation. But not just with wealthy women. The 9-to-5 girls coveted it too. Gucci's loafers were the most affordable must-have on the market. They proved so popular with middle-class shoppers that, in 1968, Aldo opened a shoe-only boutique in the St. Regis Hotel with just them in mind.

It was a business-minded move, but not just to sell more shoes: the standalone store diverted crowds away from Fifth Avenue, meaning Gucci's more regular, richer clientele could shop in peace. Really.

Gucci's loafers were as much of a hit with the boys. Frank Sinatra, Gregory Peck and Steve McQueen all had their own collections. Even George W. Bush owned a pair. If only Gucci had more to sell than just bags and shoes at the time. Now, big brands know that their accessories are gateway drugs to the rest of their racks. Gucci might have made a killing on ready-to-wear in this period from those looking for outfits to match their new shoes, but it didn't debut a collection until 1981.

Never mind. Its loafers are still the backbone of Gucci's finances. They have been stylish for as long as I have been working in fashion: in fact, I got myself a pair when I got my first proper job in journalism. That was in 2017 and, a few trips to the cobbler to be resoled aside, I still wear them. The style goes by the name Jordaan now: it has a slim shape, glossy finish and that vital horse-bit detail.

It's the one shoe you need to nail your Gucci look. And it doesn't matter that these days they aren't nearly as affordable. There are so many brilliant homages out there – these are the Gucci details and designs to look out for.

Where to begin?

Preppy types, librarians, geography teachers – perhaps even your own look when you wore school uniform. Despite the style set adopting them with such enthusiasm, it may be that you don't associate loafers with anyone stereotypically cool.

This – as with any item, in fact – is because not all loafers are created equal. A pair a fashion editor might pick will have earned its nod for its particular characteristics that a less obsessive eye might miss: the shape of the toe; embellishments; heel height, colour or finish.

Gucci is the original brand to give loafers the glossy treatment. But over the decades, the direction it has taken the shoe has changed. That's a given: to stay relevant, its stock has had to be modernised. There is not just one type of Gucci loafer now. These are the styles to know.

THE CLASSIC

Your starting point. Gucci's Jordaan loafer comes in soft, glossy leather, is slim in shape with an almond toe, and has a slight heel and gold horse-bit embellishment. Its original horse-bit loafer is just slightly squarer, with pinched stitching over the front. These timeless styles are ones to buy in black, navy, cream or brown: you can't go wrong.

THE BACKLESS

A twist on the original, Gucci's Brixton loafer has the same design as the Jordaan, but with a collapsable back heel that allows you to wear them like slippers. The Princetown, which debuted in the brand's Autumn/Winter 2015 show to rapture on the front row, is completely backless.

THE FURRY

Yes, furry: this is the backless Princetown loafer, but lined with shearling. Cosy and an instant street-style hit, though perhaps at risk of picking up more than just style points from the pavement.

THE CHUNKY

To get the look with a little more attitude, try platform loafers with chunky track soles. They make for perfect commuter – and clubbing, as nineties ravers will recall – shoes and come with a pleasing amount of height and stomp.

THE HEELED

Not everyone loves flat shoes, but those who like extra inches can still work the Gucci loafer look. Look for variations with block heels in whichever height works for you.

THE MAGPIE

Think black and brown is terribly boring? Then go for gold . . . or silver, red, pink, purple or printed. Gucci's loafers come in every colour, so don't feel you need to pick just one.

The classic

The chunky

The furry

The magpie

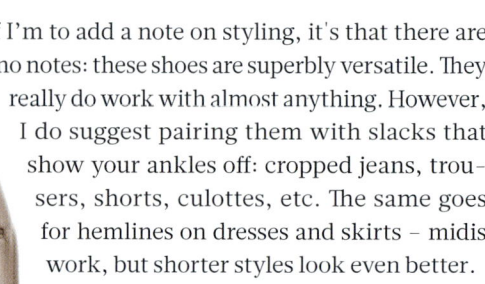

If I'm to add a note on styling, it's that there are no notes: these shoes are superbly versatile. They really do work with almost anything. However, I do suggest pairing them with slacks that show your ankles off: cropped jeans, trousers, shorts, culottes, etc. The same goes for hemlines on dresses and skirts – midis work, but shorter styles look even better.

As for socks and hosiery, go for it on the heeled styles – and I'd opt for super sheer or totally opaque. Anything else, particularly nude colours, risks looking frumpy. The flats look best with bare legs for that very reason, though I've seen them accessorised to good effect with white or black ankle socks. It's a bit schoolgirl, mind, so keep the rest of your look grown-up.

Finally: quality was everything to the Guccis, so keep your loafers polished. As ever, it is better to spend a bit more, less often. Invest in well-crafted shoes that will last longer, and get them resoled at a trusted cobbler.

When you are still pulling them out to wear years after their purchase, as I am, you know you're on to a winner.

THE
Tom Ford
ERA

3

grab
GLAMOUR

'Glamour is something more than what you put on your body. It has to do with the way you carry yourself and the impact you have on others.'

Tom Ford

By the mid-1980s Gucci had a globally recognisable logo, that cult loafer, an It-bag (thanks to one Jaque-
line Kennedy Onassis, who we'll come to later), a thriving
fragrance house and busy stores everywhere from Palm
Beach and Paris to Hong Kong and Tokyo. This was more than
enough for the majority of men in charge of the label's future.

Aldo and his sons Giorgio, Roberto and Paolo were content
to live off the fat of what was fast becoming known as Gucci's
former glories. The label had lost its luxury lustre but still
supported their glamorous lifestyles. Aldo was the man who
had taken Gucci global and nicely stuffed all their wallets, so
not only were Giorgio, Roberto and Paolo unlikely to overthrow their father, it was not in their interest to.

Only Paolo had ever really challenged him – by attempt-ing to start his own fashion label using the Gucci name in 1980. This move did not end well. He not only found himself legally banned from using the Gucci name but somewhat trapped: blocked simultaneously from doing any sincere, influential or effective work within the company or setting up on his own. He retaliated by filing evidence and testifying against his father for tax evasion in the United States. This was no private or ordinary family row.

In the eighties, Gucci became as known for its head-line-grabbing infighting as any of its fashion. Not only that, but the heavy and lucrative over-licensing of the Gucci name pioneered by Aldo meant that it was no longer associated

with exclusivity or real luxury. For the company's young-est, most ambitious shareholder, that was not good enough. Maurizio Gucci, who had inherited a 50 per cent stake in the company from his late father Rodolfo (Aldo's brother) in 1983, had plans to make Gucci great again. He would need to employ some Machiavellian tactics to get it and, ultimately, they would cost him.

This is the story of how Tom Ford came to Gucci. He is the Texan designer who took the Italian label in hand and trans-formed it into a billion-dollar brand. In his tenure as creative director, he made Gucci one of the hottest, most desirable, provocative and sexy labels in luxury fashion. Unfortunately for the family from whom the label got its name, they had absolutely nothing to do with it.

There is some Gucci dynasty drama to retrace before we get to Ford's fabulous clothes. And if you have watched Ridley Scott's 2021 film *House of Gucci*, with Adam Driver and Lady Gaga, you will not need me to recap it. But, succinctly: in 1984 Maurizio sought to take control of Gucci. He did so off the back of advice from the financial lawyer Domenico De Sole – an astute businessman already working at the heart of Gucci as secretary of the company's board of directors.

De Sole urgently felt that new leadership was needed to keep the company on track and that Maurizio should be the one to take control. This was in light of Aldo's growing list of tax evasion and fraud allegations: eventually, in 1986, he would plead guilty to non-payment of $7 million in tax and be sentenced to a year in prison. But Maurizio needed more voting power on the board to make anything happen. He went straight to the disenfranchised Paolo to get it, striking a deal that would leave his cousin with a reported $22 million and Maurizio with the faculty to overthrow his uncle.

In October 1984, that is exactly what happened. At a board meeting in New York, Maurizio was named chairman of Guccio Gucci, effectively neutering his uncle. He nominated De Sole as president of Gucci's US business, who set out to clean up the company's finances and buy back a number of franchises and licensing agreements. This, however, was far from the end of Maurizio's problems.

Maurizio relied heavily on De Sole. He had big ideas for Gucci, but lacked natural business acumen. Plus, the familial mud-slinging continued to fill gossip-page columns. Aldo and his sons – convinced that Maurizio had forged his father's pre-death signature that had sealed the handover of his Gucci shares without risk of inheritance tax, and scolded from his boardroom backstabbing – flagged their suspicions of fraud with the authorities.

That pushed De Sole and Maurizio to unceremoniously sack Aldo from the honorary presidential role he had been given in that mutinous New York board meeting. Then, in 1985, Paolo reneged on his shares agreement with Maurizio at the last minute. The same year, Maurizio's marriage to his wife Patrizia broke down completely; in December, he left her, though they would not divorce until 1994. In 1986, Aldo was sent to prison for his tax crimes and in June 1987, it was Maurizio for whom there was an arrest warrant out, for fiscal crimes of his own.

This led to Maurizio living in exile for months in Switzerland, from where he continued to run Gucci remotely. And it was during this period that he plotted in earnest to buy out his cousins, to whom Aldo had, by then, written over a significant portion of his shares. He wanted complete control of Gucci and to move it forward his way. But to do that, he needed a financial partner. Giorgio, Roberto and Paolo would never sell their precious shares to him.

Here is where the flagship bank Morgan Stanley and then lesser-known Bahrain-based financiers Investcorp, which had recently revamped Tiffany & Co, stepped in. After a meeting with Maurizio in September, the former bought

Maurizio Gucci, October 1981

Paolo out in October 1987. By the end of March 1988, Roberto and Giorgio had capitulated too. In April 1989, Aldo sold off his remaining shares in Gucci America, and the deed was done. Investcorp owned a 50 per cent stake in Gucci. Maurizio held the rest.

It does not end there, though. Nor does it end happily. In the years that followed, Maurizio all but drove Gucci into the ground, eventually forcing Investcorp to remove him as CEO. In September 1993, Maurizio signed away his remaining shares to Investcorp, leaving not a single Gucci at Gucci. Then came the bloodiest scandal in the label's history. In 1995, Maurizio was murdered: shot dead by a hitman. The prime suspect? His ex-wife Patrizia, who subsequently spent 18 years behind bars.

But before any of that happened, Dawn Mello was brought in. Maurizio, though an extravagant spender and stubborn leader, did do some good for his grandfather's label. When he set about wooing Mello, the fashion executive from New York luxury department store Bergdorf Goodman, in the summer of 1989, he changed the course of Gucci history. She was the woman who had made the formerly fusty store cool. She was also the woman who would join Gucci as creative director and usher in a talent that would turn its future around.

This talent was Tom Ford. The then little-known but ambitious Texan designer walked through Gucci's doors in 1990. He rode out those turbulent years with Mello, to whom he grew close, and by 1992, was the brand's design director. When she departed Gucci to return to Bergdorf Goodman as president in 1994, it was he who was left to run the studio.

His Autumn 1995 collection for the label is considered the one that announced his new Gucci – when the fashion world started taking note of the name Tom Ford. That same year, and 11 years after joining the company, Domenico De Sole was made Gucci's CEO.

Gucci is not one thing

Unlike Dior or Chanel, say, it does not have one set of core, signature aesthetics. Lots of looks make up Gucci's style moodboard because it has had a number of different creative heads at its helm who have each put forth their own distinct vision for the house. Tom Ford was the first, and in January 2023, the Italian designer Sabato De Sarno became the fourth.

If you had to pick one word that defined Ford's Gucci, it would be 'sex'. Va-va-voom was his trademark: from his first catwalk show for the brand – the Autumn/Winter 1994 collection – the Parsons graduate sold a seductive, flashy and desirable lifestyle that consumers gobbled up.

This is where the so-called era of 'Dom and Tom' begins. This is when Gucci becomes truly great again.

Sheer blouses. Velvet blazers. Silk shirts buttoned below the bra; eyebrow-raising low-rise hipster jeans; body-skimming bias-cut slip dresses; and GG logo G-strings styled with a sweater and ankle boots. Ford's Gucci was all glamour and a departure from the decade's trend for baggy grunge. In 1996, a *Vogue* fashion critic described Ford's Autumn 1996 collection as 'equivalent of a one-night stand at Studio 54'. That's no coincidence: in an interview with the same magazine, he said that the soundtrack in that legendary club was 'the music of my coming of age'. The whole scene behind its velvet rope is what inspired his designs; he was a regular there and he counted the glamazon Bianca Jagger as a friend.

Everyone wanted to wear Ford's Gucci. It-girl Kate Moss was a regular on his catwalks; on the red carpet, he dressed Gwyneth Paltrow, J Lo and Madonna. In 2021, Alessandro Michele, creative director of the brand from 2015 to 2023, remade the red velvet Gucci tuxedo Paltrow had worn to the 1996 MTV Video Music Awards, which she then wore to sit front row at the label's one-hundredth anniversary runway show in Hollywood. The look went viral all over again.

Ford worked at Gucci for 15 years, after which he and De Sole went on to do similarly great things at the former's own brand. He is credited with monumentally disrupting the fashion landscape, bringing hedonism and sensuality to the fore in a way no one else had before – both on the runway and off of it.

He brought in photographer Mario Testino and stylist (and later French *Vogue* editor) Carine Roitfeld to work on Gucci's wild and at times shocking advertising campaigns. These veered from artfully staged images of models who appeared like they were being groped to, in 2003, Carmen Kass pulling down her underwear to reveal pubic hair shaved into the shape of a G. None of this came without controversy: there

were calls to ban the latter ad. But it all added up to significant sales figures.

Going to such lengths – or perhaps, depths, is a better word – isn't required to embody a Ford-era Gucci look. And, look, I know sex appeal isn't top of everyone's agenda when they get dressed. The trope of 'sexy' itself can feel a bit hackneyed: it brings to mind images of red underwear and scratchy lace. No, thank you.

But let's rebrand it. Sexy can be subtle. It can also be empowering. This Gucci style principle is an attitude as much a wardrobing tip: it's about self-confidence and swagger and feeling not just comfortable but radiatingly confident in your own skin. Don't think about it in the context of dressing up for anyone else's benefit – that is what dates the concept – do it for yourself. Here are five ways how.

Show some skin

It might sound obvious, but a flash of flesh will always speak to sexiness – it's the quickest way to raise eyebrows and, if you wish, heart rates. But do not mistake that for meaning that you have to be practically naked. There are so many clever ways to do this, not so much by baring all, but rather, just a little bit. Let's break down how you might approach it, section by section.

Upper body

Perhaps you'll go sleeveless. You could wear a deep V-neck or unbutton a silk shirt low. Why not try an asymmetric neckline, or something off the shoulder – this could be a dress, top, chunky knit jumper or cardi. Feeling bolder? Sheer blouses are one route – pop one over a bralette or cami vest in the evening and show off everything and nothing at once.

Midriff

The danger zone, you might think, but it really doesn't have to be. You don't need a six pack to pull off peek-a-boo in this area – just a few clever tips.

Of course, if you've got the confidence to wear a bralette and hipsters, crack on. If not, try a high-waisted skirt or pair of trousers and find a top that is cut to crop just under your breastbone, thus revealing an alluring, but not intimidating, sliver.

See also: frocks that are cut out at the waist and left bare or are filmed over with sheer panels; they really are flattering.

Lower body

Option A: hot pants and mini-skirts.
Option B: a longer skirt or a dress with
a split hem or two. You decide.

Look for fashion you can feel

Suede! Cashmere! Feathers! Silk! The more tactile your fashion, the better when it comes to taking the Tom Ford approach to wardrobing. You want clothes that look plush and feel luxurious. Velvet and corduroy suits, silk and sheer blouses, leather and vinyl trousers and skirts, and gorgeously soft knits and furry coats all fit the bill.

Get hip

It is not the easiest look to pull off, but you can't deny Ford's love of low-rise trousers and skirts – especially if a G-string was peeping over the top. And though his hipster strides might have stereotypically come skin-tight, yours absolutely don't have to.

My advice? Try a hip-sitting pair of boyfriend jeans, i.e. those that are roomy around the rear and thighs, or a skirt worn with an oversized jacket, crisp shirt or sweater tucked just into the front waistband. Voila: you've got the look without having to worry about showing off what you ate for lunch.

Dress for disco

Shimmer, shine and sequins all capture Ford's heady Studio 54-inspired collections, so don't be afraid to wear yours day to day. The trick is in how you balance the more jazz-hands element of your outfit out. Perhaps that's something metallic on the bottom with a plain sweater or shirt on top, or a sparkly knit with jeans. Think decadence and channel your inner diva. It could even be a pair of glitzy earrings.

Ace your accessories

Go big or go home: polish your look off with seventies shades, platform shoes, chain belts and decolletage-decorating lariat necklaces. A big, bouncy blow-dry wouldn't hurt either – see chapter ten for how to do your own at home.

THE
Frida
Giannini
ERA

keep it
CHIC

'I don't like
to treat a piece
of clothing like
an object of art
because I don't
consider myself
an artist.
I'm a designer.'

Frida Giannini

Y ou probably wouldn't choose to be the designer tasked with following up Tom Ford's mammoth Gucci legacy. When he left the business acrimoniously in 2004, he was not just a designer but a celebrity in his own right – his clothes were in demand for glossy-magazine photoshoots, but so was he. In 2006, his star power was so bright that he was asked to guest edit the March issue of *Vanity Fair*. He also starred on the cover with Scarlett Johansson and Keira Knightley – who were naked. Of course!

As if his superstar personality wasn't intimidating enough for whomever had to fill the man's shoes, Ford would also be their competition. His own brand went on to be an enormous success in fashion, beauty and even film in 2009 when he wrote and directed his first movie, *A Single Man*. Decades after his first hit collection for Gucci, his name is still the last word in high-voltage glamour. In 2022, he sold his label for £2.2 billion.

So, it is just as well that the responsibility of steering Gucci post Ford fell to a woman that the designer himself had cherry-picked. Not as his successor, per se, but he did poach 24-year-old Frida Giannini from the luxury Italian label Fendi to come and work under him at Gucci in 2002. The role she filled then was head of design for handbags and accessories. By 2005, she had creative control of the entire brand.

She remained in the position until 2015. A decade is a long time in luxury fashion – not least when you consider the fact that designers at the most prestigious brands are expected to peddle out at least four collections a year. Yet Giannini, whose chunky tenure at Gucci was bookended by two megawatt creatives – Ford and her successor Alessandro Michele – might not be a name you know. That is not because the work she did at the brand was lacking. Instead, it is because she kept herself comparably behind the scenes. In an interview with *The Sunday Times* in 2007, she told the business journalist John Arlidge, 'I am not a party girl, not the PR of myself and I don't care about it.' As such, outside of the fashion industry, she was not a big name.

So what exactly defines Giannini's Gucci? The Italian from Rome, who came from a middle-class family and trained at the capital's Fashion Academy, faced plenty of criticism in her time calling Gucci's shots. Show reviews from then reveal that critics accused her collections of being too obvious, too boring, too commercial. Yet they sold well. Sales at the brand were up 16 per cent in 2006. In 2011, *The Guardian* reported that Gucci's overall profits had risen by 25 per cent during her tenure up to that point – to an estimated £660 million.

Giannini was a departure from Ford in more ways than one. She had to be if she was to take the brand forward: ready-to-wear sales had started to dip at the end of his reign and the interim creative director who replaced him, Alessandra Facchinetti, had produced collections that received some criticism. But Giannini took to the role with intent. Backstage in 2007 after revealing her latest menswear collection, she is reported to have given fighting talk to editors and buyers, declaring: 'Sex is so 1990s. I'm interested in the brain, not the body.'

Looking back at Giannini's first interviews, fashion editors often commented on the fact that she herself did not look like the Gucci sex kitten of yore. She wasn't a bleached blonde or ever heavily made-up. You would more likely find her in cashmere sweaters and metallic strappy sandals than leather trousers and vertiginous heels. It is this aesthetic shift which the designer wanted to bring to the label's catwalks, flagship stores and the rails within them.

Glamorous but grown-up: that was Giannini's Gucci. If Ford's customers shouted – about their money, sex lives and ritzy lifestyles – then Giannini wanted to find ones who would whisper. Her designs were certainly opulent, but they were also easy to wear and appealed broadly. If she used ritzy fabrics like shearling, leather or velvet, they were rendered on sporty and smart designs: sweatshirts, tailored separates and clean-line shift dresses. She often dug into archives for inspiration, leaning into various decades for each runway show. She also revived the Gucci Flora print – first on an accessories range that became a bestseller and then, in 2014 the inspiration for a garden at the highly regarded Chelsea Flower Show.

Her Gucci was aimed at the same clientele Guccio Gucci had sought out when he founded the brand: high-profile, high-net-worth types who occupied suites at The Savoy hotel. Beyoncé wore Giannini's Gucci; so did Salma Hayek. There is a recently coined term that swept social media during the last season of HBO's *Succession* in 2023, and befits her vision: 'quiet luxury'. It is an expression used to describe wardrobes filled with items that only the very wealthy will recognise for what they are: a plain T-shirt that costs hundreds of pounds; navy jumpers that, to the untrained eye, don't look any different to those sold at high-street shops – but retail for thousands.

Let's look at some of her collections to see what that means in real terms. The key adjective when describing any of Giannini's clothes is wearability. When you pick out individual pieces worn by models on her runways, that rings true.

Jennifer Lopez and Frida Giannini at the UNICEF
Women of Compassion Luncheon, February 2011

She designed for aspiration, not fantasy, and always with a modern working woman in mind. If Ford's Gucci women didn't look to have much of a life outside the bedroom, Giannini's were sitting around tables in boardrooms.

For her debut, Spring 2006, that meant deep-V rugby shirts styled with black trousers and chic cropped jackets; printed and plain flouncy chiffon frocks and knee-length city shorts. Cut to Autumn 2008 and Giannini was offering up a wardrobe suited to hippie rock chicks: shaggy luxe jackets, velvet trousers, coin belts, knee-high boots, boho blouses and suede skirts. The Spring 2011 collection was hailed by *Vogue*'s Sarah Mower as one of her best: sporty white and grey separates accompanied the sort of strappy bandage dresses that every woman wanted to go out dancing in then.

And so it goes with Giannini's work: she put clothes on the catwalk that were desirable, but not so outrageous or conceptual that they alienated potential customers. Even reviewing them with a modern eye leads you to items you would want to wear now.

Which brings us to how you can bring her look to your own wardrobe. It is not about simply copying every item she ever made. It's about distilling her principles as a designer. She was an expert in how to stand out without overtly peacocking.

Giannini's Gucci spoke to luxury shoppers who wanted to look expensive, but not try-hard. That meant no logos or flashy details. It's very easy, really, to look that well put-together. Here are my top tips to help you.

Keep it classic

You know fashion editors talk about 'classic' clothes – but what does that actually mean? To me, it translates as simple, chic items that are incredibly useful and look sharp. You can buy them on the high street, but the point is that they look high end, regardless of their price tag.

Start with a great blazer in a plain, neutral shade: you have my word, it will become the cornerstone of so many outfits. After that, more separates: a white T-shirt, plain cashmere or wool sweater, a leather jacket, a smart pair of jeans. Giannini was a master of casual luxury: her catwalks often featured denim.

When you choose these, make sure they have clean (read: unfussy) silhouettes and try to avoid embellishment. It sounds boring, but the less obvious and ostentatious detail the better here: it means that where you bought it is more likely to go undetected.

The same goes for jewellery: nothing fussy. Try hoop earrings or a chunky chain necklace.

Embrace an era

Giannini often looked to the past to inspire her, and her Gucci collections always had an era-based aesthetic. That could mean skinny jeans and big furry coats in the style of seventies glam rock, or mini-skirts, turtlenecks and knee-high boots to be a sixties mod. A sequin shift dress and heels would give a twenties nod. You could find all of these looks on her catwalks at one time or another: her work was like a cool historical dressing-up box.

Stay solid

There were plenty of prints in Giannini collections, but on the high street, solid colours tend to look more expensive. This applies to accessories as well as ready-to-wear. But by all means, embrace a full spectrum of shades: the designer was not averse to colour.

Try tonal

Saying that, consider not wearing those colours all at once. Block dressing, i.e. outfitting yourself in one colour, per Giannini's Spring 2011 show, or tonal dressing – wearing different shades of the same colour – is another great way to add value, so to speak, to your look. You can break this up with textures, too: a silk midi skirt with a knit, for example, or a black leather jacket and twill trousers. A sheer blouse with jeans would have the same effect, especially with a velvet jacket. This is super easy to do well, and a way to make any outfit more interesting.

Invest

I've said it once and I will say it again: buy less, buy better – and yes, that does occasionally mean spending a bit more. Don't be afraid to save up for a slightly pricier pair of shoes, handbag, coat or suit: if you are going to wear it again and again, it is more than worth it – and better for the planet, too.

Get the gloss

Giannini's collections always included statement pieces, but they were usually paired with items that were comparably pared back. Try that idea yourself. A shag or faux-fur jacket could look great over a suit; ditto patent or python-print knee-high boots with jeans and a blouse or a neat shift dress. As for the accessories: big shades and a smart, unbranded leather or suede bag will complete the jet-set-ic.

find your inner
EXTROVERT

'*Beauty has
no boundaries,
no rules,
no colours.*'

Alessandro Michele

H

ow long does a new designer need in order to make an impression? By which I mean, of course, a good one. For some, it might take years of trial and error on the catwalk. But the most memorable are able to do so within moments of their runway debut. Christian Dior did it with his silhouette-shifting 'New Look' in 1947. So did Alexander McQueen, with his hair-raising Jack the Ripper victim-in-spired Central Saint Martins graduation collection in 1992.

And then there is Alessandro Michele, the man who succeeded Frida Giannini at Gucci in 2015. When he was appointed its creative director, his first collection was hailed by the style set as the most exciting thing to happen in high fashion in decades, yet he had just a sliver of time to prepare for it. Forget months of careful planning. After Giannini's sudden exit from the business alongside the outgoing Gucci CEO – and her partner – Patrizio di Marco, the then unknown accessories designer had to rip up and reboot the Autumn/ Winter 2015 menswear collection in just five days.

Maverick, guru, genius and maestro. They are all words that have been used to describe Michele. You probably don't need me to tell you how influential he is. Like Ford, his name has become a brand in its own right and synonymous with his maximalist trademark style. That first collection was quite unlike anything Gucci had offered its customers before, and would shift the dial on how the world got dressed. Frilly blouses with masculine tailoring; lace peeking out from unsuspecting crew-neck knits – and berets and nerdy spec- tacles on almost every model. Michele's gender-bending, isocentric and wacky vision was clear from the off. It would define the next near decade of pop culture and style.

This, despite the fact he had less than a week to prepare for it. But reports suggest that, despite being far from a front runner – with even, in a boomerang turn, Ford's name rumoured to be in the mix to take over from Giannini – he was ready to take centre stage. Michele, who studied costume design at Rome's Academy of Costume and Fashion, had worked at Gucci for over a decade already when CEO Marco Bizzarri tapped him for the role. Ford had originally hired Michele in 2002; he went on to become an associate designer and head of accessories under Giannini.

In that role, his eye for novelty was clear, and in Gucci's design studios, he was already modelling future bestsellers. Michele, who has Messiah-like long dark hair and a beard and is often draped in jewellery, his hands covered in rings, probably wasn't easy to miss. But in interviews Bizzarri has said that Michele sealed his position as creative director thanks to what he would wear on his feet to work. One day,

Alessandro Michele (left) and Jared Leto (right)
don matching tuxes at the 2022 Met Gala, themed
'In America: An Anthology of Fashion'

Bizzarri spotted Michele shuffling around in a pair of back-less, furry loafers he had concocted. Bizarri wanted those on Gucci's catwalks – they were Princetown prototypes.

Those are just one example of how Michele could take emblems of Gucci's past and use them to drive the brand forward. He loved antiques, but had his finger well and truly on the pulse. He once said that he was interested in the past and present, but not the future. His Gucci was at once nostalgic and romantic but unequivocally modern. It didn't just nod to the agenda – it set it and appealed widely. The Princess of Wales wore Michele's Gucci; so did Billie Eilish.

Perhaps what he is best known for, though, is his rule-breaking. Michele never conformed to trends or rules when he designed. He made up his own for others to follow. His collections were gender fluid before it became trendy: he presented his first unisex show in February 2017. His playful, sexually borderless approach to wardrobing offered a new way of dressing for the very modern man – see the lace shirts, pearls and fancy flared trouser suits often modelled by the brand's long-term collaborator, androgynous heartthrob Harry Styles.

Logos weren't considered cool, so he ironically plastered T-shirts with them, making the 'GG' logo belt and 'Guccy' sweatshirts a must-have. He spliced eras and influences as he pleased, creating outfit combinations that might read as bizarre – perhaps a bit sixties, but also a bit Renaissance, with a sprinkling of mediaeval for good measure – but made the company billions. By 2018, Gucci was the hottest luxury label in the world per The Lyst Index, a quarterly report that ranks the fashion industry's most 'in' brands and products. In 2019, Anna Wintour requested that Michele co-host the industry's most exclusive night of the year with her: the Met Gala.

As for his catwalk shows, those quickly became the hottest ticket on the industry calendar, for they were known

EXQUISITE GUCCI

to be as theatrical as the clothes. No one could predict what Michele might come up with season to season; he never failed to deliver on a spectacle. For Autumn 2018, he sent models down an operating-theatre-themed runway holding figures of baby dragons, chameleons – and their own severed heads. For Spring 2022, Michele made Hollywood Boulevard his catwalk. The Spring 2023 collection was modelled by twins.

Under Michele, Gucci's celebrity pulling power peaked. The roster of A-listers he surrounded himself with was unparalleled. In his Gucci gang was the actor and musician Jared Leto, bohemian pop star Florence Welch, and Elton John, who had Michele design his farewell tour costumes. Starlet Dakota Johnson became the face of the Gucci Bloom perfume campaign in 2017; Leto and Lana Del Ray did the same in 2019 for Gucci Guilty. Michele has dressed everyone from Roger Federer to Rihanna.

He convinced starry brands to collaborate with him. Under his tenure, Gucci collaborated with Liberty, Adidas, The North Face, Disney, Xbox, The New York Yankees and even, in a surprising turn, competitor Kering-owned label Balenciaga. In his eight years as creative director, Gucci ruled. Its avant-garde runway ready-to-wear caught the attention of fashion editors, but its accessible white trainers, bum bags and branded T-shirts sold. It became the ultimate power brand.

But nothing lasts forever. Post-pandemic, Gucci's sales faltered, indicating that the popularity of Michele's aesthetic was on the wane. In 2023, it was announced that the maestro would leave Gucci, with rumours swirling that he would not bow to pressure from the boardroom to change design tack. In his place, the brand named Sabato De Sarno. His debut collection, shown at Milan Fashion Week in September 2023, departed wildly from Michele's vision: cuts were boxy, minimal and sleek. Once again, Gucci had entered a new era – but you can still dress up in a look from Michele's costume box.

If you want to have fun with fashion, there is no better muse than Michele. His time at Gucci is defined by freedom and play – he believed anyone could wear anything, so long as it gave them the power to express themselves. His Gucci was also a thinking consumer's luxury label, with collections and catwalk shows imbued with high-brow meaning and cultural touchstones – be they around identity, cinema or people. He is an artist through and through – and these are a few ways you can paint yourself in his house style.

Gender blend

Alessandro Michele is not the first designer to embrace gender fluidity in fashion, and David Bowie and Mick Jagger were outfitting themselves in flowing, feminine fabrics and jewellery long before Harry Styles stepped out in Gucci silk shirts and pearls. But Michele made it a water-cooler topic in the twenty-first century. His Gucci looks have opened up the conversation on what items get categorised as solely men and women's clothes.

Perhaps you think that's fine for rock stars, but what does it mean in an everyday wardrobe? The answer is naturally subjective to one's style. I also think it is a question that is more relevant when discussing menswear, because women have been wearing traditionally masculine tailoring for centuries: they wouldn't think twice about throwing on a blazer or pair of trousers. Plus, women are encouraged to be interested in fashion, experiment and update their looks. Men, speak-

ing generally, are under more pressure to conform.

But I think it is safe to say that we are getting more and more open-minded about how clothing is gendered. Moreover, anyone wanting to be bolder or just a bit different in their usual style, take a leaf out of Michele's book. Opt for that shirt in a bolder colour or a silkier fabric. Go for a softer silhouette or a more blouson sleeve. Have fun with accessories – there are lots of brilliant men's jewellery brands now. Look for fun prints and pair them with more understated pieces if you want to just dip your toe in. You might even want to try a statement shoe: something with a chunky sole or in a bright hue.

It is not a look you have to commit to every day; you could try it out for a party or at a festival. But know that you can, because Michele opened the world's minds up a bit – as far as he is concerned, fabulous fashion is for all.

Go geek chic

Given his love of bookish references, it is not surprising that Michele's models were so often dressed up as nerds. You might consider going full-on librarian to get his look – he was a master in what editors began to call 'granny chic'.

How? Start with a frilly buttoned-up blouse or silk shirt tucked into high-waisted trousers, a kilt or a knife-pleat midi skirt. For an extra layer: a sweater vest, cardigan or corduroy jacket. On your feet: flat or heeled loafers, brogues or Mary Jane pumps with crochet tights or knee-high socks.

Then it's all about the extras: a beret, a silk scarf knotted under the chin, costume spectacles, brooches and pearls, a neat top-handle handbag, an alice band. Voila! You're a Gucci geek – library card not included.

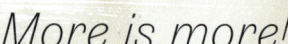

More is more!

If Coco Chanel believed you should take one thing off before leaving the house, Michele thought you should go and put five more things on. It would not be unusual for one of his show looks to consist of dresses over trousers with sweaters worn over shirts – and then belted, too, for good measure.

So more is more in the literal sense here, but also in colours and textures. Sequins and feathers, tweed and silks – they can all be worn together in Michele's world. Clashing is not a concept to be avoided; it is a way of life. There are no rules: rip up the book and go wild.

Avant-garde accessories

Are you a furry loafer or a platform pump? Maybe you prefer brightly coloured or crystal-bedecked trainers or metallic mules. Look-at-me shoes get a big tick in Michele land and are a non-committal way to make any look more interesting.

The same goes for a great bag. Michele often embroidered his, taking heritage Gucci designs and colouring them with cartoons. But you needn't go that far: just choose a style in a vibrant leather, metallic or animal print. It will instantly lift an outfit: a statement bag is the style set's secret weapon when they just fancy wearing a navy jumper and jeans.

Don't stop there: why not get yourself some oversized, sparkly sunglasses? Michele designed a number of styles inspired by Elton John. Costume jewellery and hair accessories are encouraged. Want to go further? Swap your scarf for a feather boa. Fluffy, but fabulous.

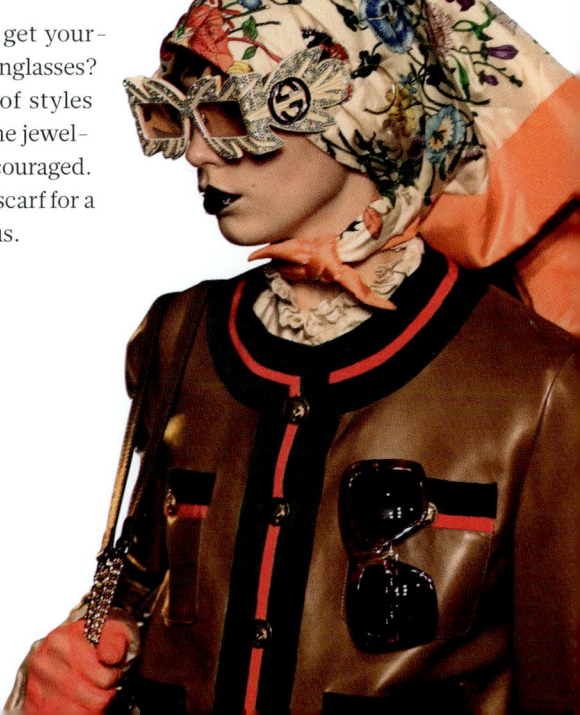

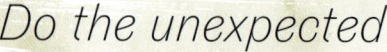

Do the unexpected

Our outfits are often what give people their first impressions of us, so why not present them with a riddle? Michele's most stellar Gucci ensemble combos worked because you would have never thought to put them together. Your aim is to look a bit wrong – but right.

Take what wardrobe consultant Allison Bornstein dubbed 'the wrong-shoe theory': it follows that an unexpected shoe pairing makes an outfit more interesting. That could be wearing a combat boot with a floaty dress, say, or a chunky loafer with a pleated midi skirt. It might be flip-flops with tailored trousers or trainers with a suit. All of these are easy to pull off and a smart trick for updating what you already have in your wardrobe without buying anything new.

As for outfit combinations, that could mean a sweater with a party skirt. You could wear a dress over a pair of trousers, a sequin bomber jacket with a shirt and tie, or a fabulous coat with sheer tights – and nothing else. And on tights and hosiery: banish plain black or nude. Michele's came in every colour, studded with crystals and in knitted patterns.

However far you take it,
do it in a way that feels like
you. Michele's Gucci was all
about self-expression. Let your
imagination run wild and step
into your own fashion fantasy.

more is
MORE

'The more
you are different,
the more
interesting.'

Alessandro Michele

You've admired the glitzy catwalk shows from afar, swooned over the gowns modelled by starlets on the red carpet and flicked through high-fashion editorials in glossy magazines. So you know that it is important for luxury brands to spotlight their clothing and that they put plenty of resources behind viral moments that, in theory, will translate to sales.

It is not wrong to assume that ready-to-wear is where Gucci and the like make most of their money. For one, there is so much of it – and why else would you create a new collection to shop every six months, if not because it was in demand? The truth is that, despite this, the majority of Gucci's consumers don't go into its stores to purchase a head-to-toe look from the shop window. If they come out with anything, it is, more likely than not, something small.

Accessories are the backbone of all luxury brand profits. Only the extremely wealthy can afford to shop for everything at high-end labels; to appeal to the rest of us and capture a young audience, a designer must be able to create super-sellable bags and shoes. Today, that means styles that appeal to the TikTok generation as much as to grown-ups. It is a challenging line to walk that Alessandro Michele in particular excelled at.

We have already covered Gucci's hit loafers and we will dig into its iconic handbag archive in a later chapter. Here, I wanted to highlight a few of its other cornerstone accessories that are worth namechecking for those hoping to create their own Gucci look.

In styling, it can be something very small that makes all the difference. You might be wearing a totally nondescript outfit (nothing wrong with that, by the way – the chicest looks often are), but just one additional flourish can give it a boost, alter how it looks to others and feels to wear. That is the joy of accessories: they pep up the ordinary. They can make you look more fashion forward without committing to a fully out-there outfit and completely change the sartorial mood of what you already own.

Cost comes into the popularity of accessories, too. Whether shopping designer or on the high street, these small items tend to have proportionate price tags compared to bigger-ticket pieces. They are, by and large, more accessible – and, as such, we feel more comfortable taking a playful approach to them, perhaps, or taking more risks. Think about it – how often do you buy a new pair of sunglasses, or treat yourself to a pair of earrings or necklace without thinking too much about how it will fit into your wardrobe? It is not unusual to have racks of belts or more than one silk scarf.

It is these items that we will discuss here. They are just a few more ways to pay homage to the brand. I will outline each below, with a little about their origin at the house and some tips on how to wear them today. These are the pieces that will work with any outfit and act as a subtle nod to the haute Italian house. Even better, they will offer the favourite pieces in your wardrobe a touch of Gucci edge.

Scarf

The Princess of Wales has worn Gucci; her late mother-in-law Princess Di was a fan too. But Gucci's first big royal connection was forged back in 1966, when Princess Grace Kelly of Monaco stepped through the doors of the brand's Milan boutique on Via Montenapoleone – and a star accessory was born.

Some stories go that the glamorous young royal was searching for a wedding gift for a friend. Others say that she was shopping for one of Gucci's hit bamboo bags. In any case, Rodolfo Gucci, then managing the boutique, wanted to ensure she left the store with a special gift, just for her.

So, he commissioned a one-off silk scarf illustrated by the Italian artist Vittorio Accornero. The print he created included 43 types of flowers, plants and insects in 37 colours. This is what went on to become Gucci's iconic 'Flora' motif, which we will delve into further in chapter nine.

Silk scarves have been stocked at Gucci ever since. Alessandro Michele knotted them around the necks and heads of his granny-chic catwalk and campaign models; the hip-hop star A$AP Rocky tied one around his head and under his chin, in the style of Queen Elizabeth II, on the red carpet in 2018. Today, this delicate item comes in all varieties of prints and colours – and there are so many ways to pull it off.

1

You could go the way of A$AP

Fold the scarf in half, corner to corner, wrap it around your head and knot the long ties under your chin. This is a nice idea on a windy day – or in a convertible, with chic cat-eye shades – but can veer into *The Crown* costume territory if paired with a quilted jacket or Barbour.

Consider wearing it around your neck

2

Knot it slightly to the side, Grace Kelly style; tie it as a cravat with a shirt or even fold it in half, into a triangle, and drape it over your shoulders on top of a jumper or blazer. This is handy during in-betweeny months, where temperatures call for what fashion editors refer to as 'transitional dressing'.

3

Alternatively, pop it in your hair

Fold it to ruler width and wear it as an alice band, or tie it around your ponytail.

One more idea

4

Knot it over the strap of your favourite handbag. The act will give your old faithful new life.

Belt

Before there were It-bags, there were belts. The first Gucci belt was designed by Guccio back in 1933 and it has maintained its desirability through the decades: in 2018, the GG-logo Marmont style was named the most-wanted product by the global shopping data platform Lyst. That is probably the version you are most likely to recognise; it has been worn by everyone from Jennifer Aniston to Cindy Crawford.

The brand makes plenty of non-branded belts too. These are luxury takes on what you might consider to be an essential accessory in your wardrobes. But you don't need an expensive version, nor to see it just as something to keep baggy trousers up. Belts can do so much more than that.

A belt can break up an outfit or create a waist – look for your slimmest point and fasten it there. It can be thread through trouser or skirt loops, but also over coats, blazers, and even a dress. You might consider trying a corset belt for a more dramatic look.

Look for neutral styles – black, beige, white or navy – but experiment with your belts, too. They are as much a statement-maker as a bag or shoe. Try styles in Gucci red or green, or go metallic with silver or gold. A statement buckle is a fun eye-draw, too: look for those in gold or silver, which come crystal or pearl-studded for a Gucci look.

Sunglasses

We know that Gucci is equal to glamour, and what oozes mystique more than a sleek pair of shades? Any number of styles fits the bill by the brand's house codes. Let's look at which might best suit your face.

ROUND FACES

Look for square or rectangular frames and avoid any with soft lines. You are looking for styles with sharp edges, but beyond that they can be any shape.

SQUARE FACES

Try round and rimless shapes – anything oval, circular or with soft edges will suit this face shape.

HEART-SHAPED FACES

Sunglasses that mimic the dimensions of your face are best: i.e. those that are wider at the top and narrow at the bottom: think aviators (very Maurizio Gucci) or cat eyes (a la Grace Kelly).

OVAL FACES

Give oversized frames a go, which will give the illusion of width. These can be any shape.

Round faces

Square faces

Oval faces

Heart-shaped faces

Jewellery

Jewellery: your fastest and easiest outfit diversifier. Even if you
change nothing else season to
season, just pivoting what earrings
you plug into your lobes will
alter how those love-worn pieces
look and feel. But which gems best
communicate Gucci's aesthetic?

GOLD CHAINS

These are a great place to start. It was Frida Giannini who transformed the Gucci horse-bit into bracelets and necklaces, but any of the plethora of chain necklaces and bracelets available on the high street and contemporary demi-fine jewellery brands would act as a suitable nod. These are fantastically simple, stylish and versatile items, so much so that you may find you never take yours off.

HOOP EARRINGS

Ditto: there is a reason fashion editors consider them practically a uniform. They are understated but classic, go with everything and easily look expensive. Look for the small- to medium-sized styles and try mixed-metal, twisted or chunky designs for something different.

COSTUME JEWELLERY

This also comes Gucci approved, if we are to take the Michele approach. His more-is-more aesthetic applied to the gems he crafted, too: think crystal animal pendants and wildlife motifs, huge pearl string necklaces with outsize crystal-studded GG and crucifix pendants and cascading rhinestone chandelier earrings. The zanier the better, here: have fun.

A final note:
don't limit yourself
to decorating
in the obvious places.
Try hair clips and
brooches too.

GIDDY UP

'*Fashion is the most beautiful illusion you can have.*'

Alessandro Michele

Riding boots and hard helmets; harnesses, horse-bit hardware and smart dressage jackets. Standard uniform on the eventing circuit? Yes. But in 2021, they were also part of eccentric outfit combinations on a Gucci catwalk.

The brand was showcasing that year's Autumn/Winter collection by Alessandro Michele. When he put that show together to kick off Gucci's centenary celebrations, the format might have been liberal compared to a standard runway – it was delivered virtually, in film form, thanks to the Covid-19 pandemic – but the equine influences were all too literal. That's because they go back to Gucci's very beginnings. Well, sort of.

Grab your crop and saddle up: this section of the brand's journey is to be taken on horseback. It is well documented that Gucci has long-standing equestrian links. Its most famous products bear snaffle horse-bits and its trademark colours were originally inspired by girth straps. Exactly why, though, is an excellent story – and one Aldo Gucci would have preferred that the truth didn't get in the way of.

We already know how ambitious Aldo was for Gucci. That's no bad thing, of course, but it did mean he was known to embellish where he deemed necessary, if it benefitted the brand. This is not unusual behaviour among those hoping to sell a dream: Coco Chanel was famous for taking liberties with the truth in regard to her own humble background. But on the subject of Gucci and horses, Aldo fabricated an entire myth. He told anyone who asked that the family had a rich tradition of saddle making.

His version of Gucci family history is a lovely one. Aldo impressed upon customers, journalists and buyers that the Guccis had crafted saddles for nobility in mediaeval courts. This, he said, was why the world of horse riding is so strongly communicated in Gucci products. He even displayed riding accessories in boutiques to prop up the story, a tactic so successful that eventually many Gucci employees and even the Guccis themselves believed it.

It was a savvy move that endeared Gucci to the elite consumers Aldo was hoping to attract. But the truth behind the label's hankering for all things horsey is that his father Guccio was originally drawn to the sport's aesthetic because it was aspirational. He picked up that the keeping, racing and admiration of horses was a wealthy man's hobby during his time working at The Savoy. That's why Gucci's earliest leather creations were indeed saddles and saddlebags – but in the 1920s, not fourteenth century.

Equestrianism remains one of the label's strongest house codes. Casting an eye back on Gucci collections over the decades proves just how many ways it has been interpreted. Saddle shapes have appeared on several handbags: in 2023, one such style, the Horsebit 1955, was reissued in an asymmetric saddle-esque shape for a new generation. Its stable-centric hardware, the horse-bit clasp, is used liberally across ready-to-wear, handbags, jewellery and shoes.

The green and red webbed stripes have been appropriated not just on luggage and straps but as patterns on clothing: in Sabato De Sarno's debut collection, he placed them on coordinating python jackets, hot pants and platform horse-bit loafers. It is perhaps Michele, though, who took the concept furthest. In that aforementioned 2021 collection, he designed a leather headpiece inspired by riding helmets and harnesses, complete with a real horsehair Mohican that enraged animal rights organisations.

Your approach doesn't have to be quite so extreme. An equestrian aesthetic is easy to achieve. Let's trot through a few ways one might work a Gucci-inspired approach to it into an everyday wardrobe – without scaring the horses.

Get hot for horse-bit

It's a piece of metal hardware straight from the horse's mouth, and it's no secret that Gucci is the brand which made the horse-bit snaffle haute. These days, it is easy to spot across brands in every price bracket.

It is the most effortless way to inject your wardrobe with some horsepower. Just pick up a handbag or pair of shoes – any style, not just loafers – with the chain-link detail. Bracelets, belts and necklaces commonly come in horse-bit designs too, and are a subtle way to pay homage.

Reach for riding boots

Stylish and practical don't always go hand-in-hand on high-fashion runways, but you can't say that about Gucci's riding boots. The flat, sturdy knee-high footwear is made for walking and looks fantastic with jeans, under midi skirts and frocks or with short hemlines. You don't have to go to an equestrian specialist to find them; most brands stock a style every season. It is timeless.

Michele's interpretation for Autumn 2021 came in black and burgundy with a harness across the ankle, but iterations in plain black or shades of brown, navy or dark red fit the bill. You want a pair in glossy leather rather than suede, and the zip should run up the inside. And remember, fashion's riding boots are for keeping clean – don't go mucking out the stables in them.

Get go-faster stripes

If you want two colours that exemplify Gucci, they are green and red – and not just because of the label's Italian roots. These are the shades that have been banded together in stripes across every type of Gucci product, in the style of those saddle straps Guccio regularly ported at The Savoy. They are as recognisable as its logo.

For the British aristocrats who owned them, it is said that red echoed the shade of their fox-hunting jackets, while green symbolised wealthy owners of the countryside. But another story goes that Gucci's signature deep, almost burgundy, hue is inspired by something else at the luxury hotel: its elevator, in which Guccio Gucci worked.

At the time, it was the first electric lift in London and took a whole seven minutes to reach the top floor.

Because of that, and the immense anxiety guests had in using it, the hotel's owner had it painted red like an opera house and decked out with plush leather banquettes. Busboys would serve drinks and smelling salts; relaxed by the remedies on offer, those punters would chat freely to the hotel staff. One can imagine Guccio learned a lot there. It was called the Ascending Room.

Both colours are easy to work into an outfit, despite what you might think about their festive connotations. I would advise seeking out singular items that incorporate both colours and can be paired with a different shade in the rest of your outfit – for example, a striped jumper paired with something plain on bottom.

Jump into jodhpurs

Allow me some artistic licence here, because I am swapping out actual skin-tight riding trousers for their even stretchier cousins: leggings. This item is no longer just for the gym – it looks great as part of dinner, drinks and dancing outfits too. It was 2016 when British *Vogue* dictated that the stretchy, clingy strides would break out of the loungewear department, and the style set has adopted them on the front row ever since.

Stirrup styles which hook around the foot are particularly popular and fit perfectly in our stable of equine looks. Fashion editors treat them as interchangeable with their black trousers and jeans. Leggings are a cornerstone of modern wardrobes now. You can dress them up as easily for a night out as you can a dog walk.

For the latter, it is best to do so with something oversized. Doing so will balance out your silhouette – and, if desired, cover your bum.

Look for pieces on the smarter side that will counter any feeling of slouch. Try a crisp XXL boyfriend shirt, an outsize blazer (you could belt it), your leather jacket or a chunky, polished knit.

On your feet, go with boots, heels, loafers or ballet pumps. Trainers are fine but must feel equally uptown, i.e. in leather or suede – and clean.

Bank on a blazer

Hurrah: your blazer fits into this category – showjumpers often wear them at events. Waisted iterations that sit no longer than the hip and come with gold buttons are on the nose. But the one in your wardrobe will do.

bag
BRILLIANCE

'*Clothes are endless possibilities for meaning because with every change or different association, you are a different person.*'

Alessandro Michele

E

lizabeth Taylor liked to hang them over the crook of her elbow; Audrey Hepburn preferred to clutch hers by hand. Princess Di loved one style so much the brand eventually named it after her. The same can be said for Jackie O.

Gucci's handbags are some of the twentieth century's most iconic – in no small part because they have held the wallets, lipsticks and keys belonging to equally legendary women. It is no secret that high-profile clientele boost a brand's credibility, but in this regard, Gucci's accessories department has particular form. From tasteful totes to cult-worthy shoulder bags, the label has always been a certified arm-candy factory. Its portable creations aren't just devoured by global tastemakers but proudly displayed, too.

It has never had a problem seducing the era's brightest stars. Like every other brand, it makes a point of securing and showcasing its cosy relationships with them. Ford dressed everyone from Demi Moore to Nicole Kidman; Michele transformed modern menswear through his creative collaboration with the megawatt musician Harry Styles. In October 2023, Sabato De Sarno wasted no time in setting up his own attention-grabbing alliance: just months after coming on board as creative director, he launched a new handbag and campaign with the Gen Z pop pin up Billie Eilish.

Look back, though, and you'll find that Gucci has nurtured links to Hollywood since the fifties. The Swedish starlet Ingrid Bergman clutched its handbags in her films *Stromboli* (1950), *Europa '51* (1952) and *Viaggio in Italia* (1954). A house friendship with the Italian director Michelangelo Antonioni bagged the brand screen time throughout the sixties. Most recently, it became the subject of a feature film itself: Lady Gaga, Adam Driver, Jared Leto and Al Pacino starred in 2021's epic *House of Gucci*.

In real life (sort of), deciding who Gucci dresses is something an entire in-house VIP team puts its energy into. But, earlier, Guccio and his scions realised that selling a bag, shoe or bottle of perfume was as much about selling the dream of emulating the individual in possession of it. Hepburn, Taylor and Sofia Loren are among the earliest silver-screen starlets who embraced the label's accessories. Two of its It-bags are even named after particularly well-known – and well-dressed – customers: the 'Jackie' shoulder bag and 'Diana' tote were first thrust into the spotlight by their notable owners in the sixties and nineties, respectively, but are still bestsellers.

It goes without saying that a designer bag should give glamour. But in a world where luxury-accessory blueprints are increasingly influenced by how the finished item will

Jacqueline Kennedy Onassis with the original
Gucci saddlebag in New York in 1970

look on social media, rather than hung on an individual's shoulder, Gucci's icons in this department feel pleasingly old school. Far from being gimmicky, the word that really comes to mind when you study them is 'classic'. The leather and canvas is sleek, the designs are clean and the proportions are sensible – not always a given.

Don't mistake that description for staid. With their curves and chic hardware, Gucci bags are quite sexy. They often possess an understated va-va-voom. In their carefully stitched leather or canvas shapes, there is the Florentine craftsmanship that the house has always prided itself on. Their designs have aged well, but that's not the only reason that Gucci bags are the sort which look better the longer you own them. The fact that well-worn iterations remain desirable through the decades speaks to the phrase Aldo Gucci reportedly used when justifying the brand's costs: that quality is remembered long after the price is forgotten.

They come in all shapes and sizes. To my mind, there are five you really need to know. Below, I have detailed their stories and characteristics, so you can spot them in the wild – and find a version of your own.

1

The Bamboo

They're not just design quirks: the distinctive curved real-bamboo handle and twist clasp of this polished purse, first conceived in 1947 by Guccio Gucci, came out of both creativity and necessity due to material shortages during the Second World War. Bamboo could be easily imported from Japan, and once it arrived at Gucci's workshops, it was shaped and lacquered by its artisans by hand – in a method that is now patented by the company. As for the bag's shape, it was originally saddle-inspired; now, the demure design is fitting for ladies who lunch.

Shape
semi-circle

Size
small

How to carry
handheld or cross body

Finish
bamboo handle, twist clasp and gold chain

Shape
hobo

Size
medium
to large

**How
to carry**
on the shoulder

Finish
golden clasp

2

The Jackie

When Jackie Kennedy Onassis stepped out with Gucci's Fifties Constance unisex tote in 1961, the brand knew it had to capitalise on the inevitable demand that would follow, so it swiftly renamed the slouchy shoulder bag after the all-American influencer. Jackie O, then First Lady of the United States, was the most stylish woman in the world at the time and her endorsement of the 'hobo' holdall did indeed cause a run (and by the way, if that descriptive term is jarring, know that it is a dated categoriser, but still one used to identify this particular bag shape). It has been revisited by several of Gucci's designers, Tom Ford and Alessandro Michele included. Giannini made Kate Moss the face of her soft, roomy leather take on it in 2014. Now it comes in every kind of colour and size, from classic leather to crystal-studded mesh and faux fur.

3

The Diana

It was simply known as the bamboo tote, first designed in the 1980s, when she styled it with smart frocks and jeans alike. But in 2021, Alessandro Michele renamed Princess Diana's favourite Gucci bag for her on what would have been her sixtieth birthday. This practical, classic tote comes in structured square, soft and bucket shapes now, but always has that unique wooden handle.

Size
large

Shape
tote

How to carry
handheld or over the crook of the elbow

Finish
bamboo handle

Shape
camera bag

Finish
plain smooth or
grain leather;
leather strap

**How
to carry**
cross body

Size
small

4

The Soho

Simple yet superb for going out-out, Gucci's Soho Disco is a small, rectangular camera bag conceived by Frida Giannini in 2012. Her iteration, an instant hit, came in grainy plain leather, embossed with the interlocking 'GG' logo; in 2022, the model evolved: it goes by 'Blondie' and has diagonal, quilted stitching.

Shape
flap bag

Size
medium

Finish
horse-bit hardware
with a leather, chain
or fabric strap

**How
to carry**
cross body or
on the shoulder

5

The Horsebit

It's not just loafers that Aldo decorated with that horse-bit hardware: in 1955, the embellishment made it onto the brand's handbags, too. Tom Ford was the first to put his spin on it, enlarging the horse-bit to XXL proportions on his Horsebit Chain Bag for Autumn 2003, a design that was reissued 20 years later. Michele debuted a preppy take in 2020: a structured, shiny, smooth leather flap bag you could easily fit a diary or book in. In 2023, De Sarno pivoted the design again to celebrate its seventieth anniversary, this time reinventing the Horsebit with an asymmetric silhouette that incorporates sustainable materials.

Now you know what styles of bag to look for, let's go through a few tips for handbag buying generally. If you're someone who doesn't invest in a new model very often, it is important to get it right – this is likely to be something you use every day.

1 Look for something without a logo

I see lots of lovely, affordable bags that could easily pass for something more expensive – were it not for the fact that its origins are clearly marked on the front. Plus, most of Gucci's greatest bags began life unbranded, recogniz-able only to those who knew what they were. When in doubt, remember that understated is always tasteful.

Quality matters

That doesn't mean you have to buy real leather – vegan options are fantastic now – but look for simple, well-made designs that you can see surviving wear and tear. You want your bags to age well. Saying that, you might consider choosing one which already has.

Try an independent brand

I love the high street, truly, but there are so many excellent boutique labels making reasonably priced, high-quality handbags. Some even make their wares in the same factories as luxury designers. At the very least, you could find those which, like Gucci's, are Made in Italy.

Look for verified vintage

Lots of online pre-loved platforms have systems in place for identifying fakes now; alternatively, locate a local vintage expert who can source the specific style you are looking for.

pick your
PRINT

'Never, ever,
ever wear
anything you
are uncomfortable
in. Because that
is what you'll
project: "I look
like a fool."'

Tom Ford

One was commissioned on the finest silk for a princess, the other was originally designed on a wartime austerity-friendly hemp. Both have stood the test of time as aesthetic pillars at Gucci, but which will prove to be your preferred look of these two iconic prints?

Not that you have to choose. I just think you might prefer one over the other. Gucci's Diamante and Flora motifs both qualify as its signatures, for they have proved to be truly timeless, but they are very different. The former is minimalist, repetitive, geometric and comes in shades of beige. The latter bursts forth from whatever item it is on: it is a vivid riot of colour, flowers and insects that look almost alive. I would be surprised if both appealed equally to an individual's tastes.

Both were conceived while the Gucci family was still steering the brand creatively. The brown-on-brown Diamante motif was first designed by Guccio in the 1930s, and later tweaked by his sons to include the label's GG monogram. Flora, as we touched on in chapter six, was the work of Italian artist Vittorio Accornero, commissioned by Rodolfo Gucci on a scarf for Princess Grace of Monaco in 1966.

But before knowing all that, could you have instantly traced both back to the Italian label? My bet would be that you'd recognise the Diamante as Gucci offspring, but perhaps not its fancy floral sibling. The Diamante has been synonymous with Gucci since its very beginnings. What began as a solution to material shortages during the Second World War has gone on to be one of, if not the, most significant Gucci markers.

These days you can find it on shoes, bags – even baseball caps. It is pressed onto the label's designer wristwatch faces and has been plastered on its phone cases. From the Ford era through to De Sarno's creative reign, it has been reprised on leather bomber jackets and blazers – knickers, tights and tops, too.

It has certainly bagged an upgrade from the modest material it started life on. Guccio first designed his diamante print for luggage – then simply a series of small diamonds arranged in criss-crossing horizontal lines to create a larger diamond pattern, rather than with the added intersecting GG logos it has now – in the middle of the Second World War. Italy was under Mussolini then. It was in alliance with Nazi Germany, too. So it is not that surprising that the League of Nations imposed sanctions on the country's trade, but it was inconvenient for Guccio Gucci, novice luggage mogul. It meant there was a scarcity of what he needed most: leather.

No matter. In a show of resourcefulness, he found a plain woven hemp from Naples and stitched onto it his new signa-

ture print. It was intended to set Gucci apart from its compet-
itors, and it worked. The pattern as it exists now – and has
done since the sixties – is one of the most distinguished in
luxury fashion.

Flora is famous too, of course, but I'd argue it is less ubiq-
uitous. It is also, simply because it doesn't incorporate a logo,
less obviously Gucci. But this 37-colour pattern, made up of
43 varieties of flowers, plants and bugs, has flourished far
beyond that first scarf designed for Princess Grace.

Frida Giannini was particularly fond of Flora: it was the
first print she plucked from the archives and revived across
her collections. Michele played around with it too, once
layering it up, in fact, with the Diamante. Bold.

The floral print has sprouted outside of Gucci's fashion
department. There have been Flora-related beauty launches
and cultural partnerships, too. One such collaboration is
Gucci's 2014 garden at the RHS Chelsea Flower Show in the
UK. At that annual – and quite posh – pop-up in London, the
brand brought the Flora print to life with the award-win-
ning landscape and garden designer Sarah Eberle. Another
is the Flora perfume (surprise: it's floral!) commissioned by
Giannini in 2009 and, at the time of writing, advertised by
the pop star Miley Cyrus.

Styling your print

Having got to grips with your Gucci motifs, you might be wondering how best to wear them. There are basic tips and tricks for styling prints (pair with plain; start small with accessories; use tactfully in an outfit to draw the eye), but in this case I am not going to dish out my usual advice. The Diamante and the Flora are unique. I think they require special treatment.

Let me explain. Often, but not always, prints can be overpowering in an outfit. Leopard, for example, comes with all sorts of various connotations: you might not wish to wear it head to toe. I don't think this applies to the Diamante print, nor to the Flora. You could easily wear an entire ensemble of both and not feel as though it was too much.

I think this is especially true when you consider the fact that Gucci's Diamante is embossed subtly as often as it is boldly. You might find it in crystal form on a pair of black slingbacks, say, or in shades of cream on beige on a handbag. Sometimes it is even impressed upon leather or suede, so that it is almost invisible. Something to consider.

As for the Flora, it is, ultimately, florals. It may not be ditsy, but it is still in the family of one of the most popular prints in womenswear. If that pretty aesthetic is your thing, then it is easy to adopt: approach with extreme confidence. Look for large painterly floral patterns on negative space in white, black, navy or red. Extra points for creepy crawlies: butterflies, etc.

Another marker of difference with these prints is that the Diamante incorporates the Gucci logo. Now, how best to appropriate that into a more affordable look? I would never recommend buying a fake, so one route is to forget the 'GG' element entirely and look for items that come in a simple geometric diamond print. Another is to source the real thing – not from a Gucci boutique, but second-hand.

Stay with me. It might not be as expensive or tricky as you think. Here are some tips from Heartleigh Little, a New York City-based stylist and vintage collector who has made a career out of sourcing the best pre-loved luxury goods. She has her own boutique (follow @heartandlous on Instagram) but says her favourite place to shop vintage is in Paris. I know – how fabulous.

DON'T ASSUME THAT
SECOND-HAND MEANS PAYING LESS

While I do love a thrifty find, I really appreciate curated vintage. You're paying a premium, but for good reason.

AUTHENTICITY IS TRICKY

Usually this will be reflected in the price and a reputable shop. Do your research.

BEWARE FAKES

If you think it's too good to be true, it probably is. Always run your purchase through a third-party service if you have doubts. Most online platforms like Vestiaire Collective, Vinted and even eBay now have this built in.

HOP ONLINE

The best platforms to currently shop second-hand designer are The Real Real, Vestiaire Collective, Vinted, Depop and eBay.

HIT THE CHARITY SHOPS
IN AFFLUENT AREAS

You don't need me to point out that the quality of the cast-offs will be better when they have come from homes with walk-in wardrobes. It might just be where you find your very own precious piece of Gucci.

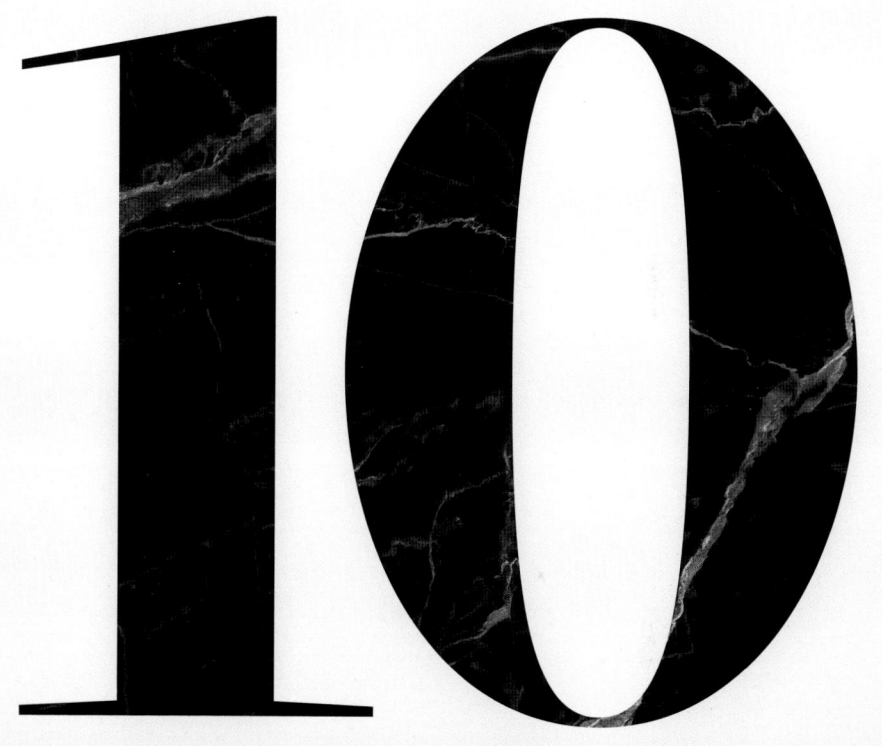

10

bold
BEAUTY

'For me, beauty
and fashion are
always connected.
One doesn't exist
without the other.'

Frida Giannini

Glamorous, gorgeous, glossy, Gucci – but, in this chapter, not for your wardrobe. In this final section, we are going to explore how to get the Italian super-brand's look from your beauty cupboard. Here, step inside the world of Gucci cosmetics with me.

Consider these your finishing touches. You've nailed the shoes, the bags and the clothes – but, listen, you can actually oomph up your look every day, Gucci-style, even without any of that. The label's aesthetic influence extends well beyond clothing. What you wear on your cheeks, eyes and lips – even how you style your hair – can incorporate some Gucci cool, too.

What that is, exactly, has naturally evolved through its many eras. When a creative director ushers in their aesthetic vision, it applies to a full look: from blow-dried head to pedicured toe. Yet what Gucci has always been synonymous with is polish. The brand evokes allure and aspiration and, with that in mind, I think it encourages an unapologetic approach to grooming. Forget barely-there make-up and bedhead: Gucci customers, VIPs and even shop-floor staff are not afraid to look like they have made an effort.

Gucci has been selling perfume since the seventies. It launched a cosmetics line in 2014, then revamped it in 2019. Today, the @guccibeauty Instagram has millions of followers; its collection of lipsticks, foundation and eyeshadows come encased in glistening gold palettes. These are the most affordable items sold by Gucci, but that is not the only reason they are so popular. Gucci's make-up has been lauded by beauty editors, who think that the products really work.

You don't have to invest in those to bring a little Gucci to your morning routine. I spoke to a panel of experts on how they would approach it. Let's start with your complexion.

The glow

Fake tan is not everyone's cup of tea, but you can't beat it for added radiance – if done well. Park nightmarish visions of overdone orange and streaky limbs: I'm thinking of Tom Ford's models here, whose flesh often glistened, but also of the celebrities sitting on Gucci's front row who wouldn't even consider leaving the house without a precisely applied spray tan.

James Harknett is a wizard on this topic. Known as the 'Tom Ford of tanning' (how apt), he has won awards for his brilliant bronzing and applied it to the likes of Spice Girl Geri Halliwell and supermodel David Gandy. On the next page, he shares his top tips for getting your own faux glow at home.

Step-by-step

There are so many innovative products right now which complement our favourite formulas, so there really is something to suit every type of complexion, and how you prefer to tan. The best new formulas don't just deliver beautiful tans – they are also there to really care for and protect the skin's precious barrier. For facial tanning, mists and sprays work well as they are superlight on the skin. Look on the back of the bottle and avoid ingredients which are not helpful to skin health: mineral oils, amyl acetate, octyl stearate, parabens, alcohol and artificial fragrances. Anything which is synthetic, sits on the skin or is a known irritant is a no-no.

If you are planning to tan before an event, **do it the day before**. This allows the self-tan to really develop overnight. For weddings, brides like to tan 48 hours before for a really subtle finish.

My tips for the perfect tan start with **good old-fashioned body prep**. A few days before you plan your application of self-tanner, start by smoothing out the skin with an exfoliating glove. Concentrate on areas that get a build up of cells, such as under the breasts and on strap lines. These are common areas where tan often clings to.

Ensure any hair removal is done well before you tan – 24 hours or more is best for shaving. If it's a leg or body wax, then make it 48 to 72 hours. The skin can then renew evenly and the self-tan has enough cells to bind with to allow the tan to react.

I always recommend working in a **cool bathroom: no humidity**. Also, tanning in front of a mirror will help. Before any tan hits the skin, ensure hair is tied back, a little Vaseline is spread over the brows to avoid dye collecting in them and all your jewellery is removed. It's also a good idea to throw down a towel, especially if your chosen tan is a mist.

Next, **moisturise the parts of the body that self-tan grabs to**: the heels, kneecaps, elbows, hands and tops of feet. A little moisture will barrier the skin to allow for natural results.

'If you want to achieve a natural look as much as possible, assess your own skin tone without any sun exposure. Once you know that, then it's pretty simple to choose a product to achieve the most flawless finish to work with your skin, rather than against it.'
James Harknett

Start with the legs first.
Standing up, bend the knee by lifting it, to open the creases in the front of the knee. If you're using a mousse, round circular motions allow a smooth, even and fast application.

My top tip is **use the remnants of tan left on your mitt over the hands and feet**. Less is more in these areas. If using a tanning mist, three quick, short bursts will be enough to give a lovely glow.

Once you have achieved the self-tan you want, then it's time to enhance it without spoiling your hard work! Step away from heavy foundation and allow your skin to breathe and glow. **Try a lightweight skin tint for your face, a shimmer dry oil on the body or a highlighter across your cheekbones and décolletage**.

The glam

Now, on to make-up. I am someone who advocates a subtle look for daytime, but after dark, all bets are off. I asked the celebrity make-up artist Julia Wren (who you can follow on @juliawrenmakeup_tutorials) how to get the ultimate Gucci going-out beauty look. This is her guide to the perfect complexion, smokey eye and bold lip.

FACE

Always start with fresh skin: exfoliated, hydrated and primed. My tip for that extra glow is to use two different highlighters. Firstly, use a cream or gel highlighter on your cheekbones before your foundation, then, for a supercharged shine, add a dusting of highlight powder to finish off the look.

EYES

The easiest way to a modern smokey eye is to use an eyeshadow stick: they are so easy to blend with a brush or even your finger and come in so many colours. Define the waterline with a waterproof pencil to add extra drama, add a full coating of mascara, lashes if you dare – and you're done.

LIPS

Begin by using a lip scrub for the smoothest lips; if you don't have one in your make-up bag, then some balm and a toothbrush will make do. My number-one tip is to use a lip liner, not just on the edge of your lips, but all over. Liners have great staying power so will help to keep your lips looking fresh all night long. Use a liner as near in colour to your lipstick as you can find, and top up through the night with the lipstick.

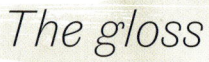

The gloss

A great blow-dry can cover all manner of sins, but it is also a shortcut to feeling just a bit more together. I think the key is to try and achieve a hairstyle that is both glossy and a bit undone. For this, I turned to the celebrity hairdresser George Northwood (@georgenorthwood on Instagram) who, opposite, details how to give yourself gently glamorous tresses at home.

If you want to cheat, though, I recommend a rotating blow-dry brush. And don't forget the dry shampoo to make it last longer: try applying it the night before. The best blow-dry could last up to three days.

The best way to get a sexy blow-out is to start off with some volumising spray and apply that to towel-dried hair.

Then tip your hair upside down and blast lots of heat into it with a hairdryer, stretching it at the roots.

When your hair is 60 to 70 per cent dry, flip it up and, with a big round brush, wrap the hair around the brush, section by section and roll it as you would a roller and apply heat to it.

Hold this position for a bit and then twist it out and leave it. Then work your way around the entire head.

Finish off by shaking it through to make it look less coiffed. Perhaps add some moisturising cream or hairspray of your choice.

There we have it, a little Gucci tool kit. You have everything you need now to bring a little bit of the Italian label's style to life in your own wardrobe. If you are to take one final note away, let it be to do it in your own way. Each main character in Gucci's story has been an individualist. They knew the power of harnessing their own look. Take each of these style principles and make them your own.

Ciao!

Guccio Gucci
1881–1953
m. Aida Calvelli

Ugo
1889–1973
(son of Aida)

Grimalda
1903–1989
m. Giovanni Vitali

Enzo
1904–1913

Patricia
(1963)
[with Bruna Palombo]

Giorgio
1928–2020
m. Orietta Mariotti
m. Maria Pia

The GUCCI *family tree*

Aldo	Vasco	Rodolfo
1905–1990	**1907–1974**	**1912–1983**
m. Olwen Price	*m.* Maria Taburchi	*m.* Alessandra
m. Bruna Palombo		Winkelhauser Ratti
		(Sandra Ravel)

Paolo	Roberto	Maurizio
1931–1995	**1932–2009**	**1948–1995**
m. Yvonne Moschetto	*m.* Drusilla Cafferelli	*m.* Patrizia Reggiani
m. Jenny Garwood		
Penny Armstrong		

References

Articles

Arlidge, John. 'G Force', thetimes.co.uk, 2007

Cartner-Morley, Jess. 'The Story of Gucci', theguardian.com, 2011

Murphy, Anna. 'Gucci creative director Alessandro Michele has stepped down – why', thetimes.co.uk, 2022

Murphy, Anna. 'How A-list women fell for the new guy at Gucci ', thetimes.co.uk, 2016

Royce-Greensill, Sarah. 'Gucci to design Flora garden at Chelsea Flower Show', fashion.telegraph.co.uk, 2014

'Gucci Fall 1996 Ready-to-Wear Collection', vogue.com, 1996

Books

Forden, Sara Gay. *The House of Gucci: A Sensational Story of Murder, Madness, Glamour, and Greed*. Kindle Edition, Custom House, 2012

Homer, Karen. *Little Book of Gucci*, Welbeck, 2020

Quote sources

p.22 Gucci, Aldo. Available from: quote-fancy.com/quote/1574586

p.30 Gucci, Aldo (cited by Sara Gay Forden in *The House of Gucci: A Sensational Story of Murder, Madness, Glamour, and Greed*. Kindle Edition, Custom House, 2012)

p.46 Ford, Tom. Available from: goalcast.com/tom-ford-quotes/

p.68 Giannini, Frida (as cited by Anamaria Wilson in 'Frida Giannini: A Fashionable Life', harpersbazaar.com, 2011)

p.86 Michele, Alessandro. Available from: brainyquote.com/authors/alessandro-michele-quotes

P.106 Michele, Alessandro (as cited by Robin Givhan in 'Beyoncé loves his work. So does Melania. Meet the Gucci designer trying to bridge many divides', washingtonpost.com, 2017)

p.124 Michele, Alessandro (as cited by Zach Baron in 'Praise Be Alessandro Michele, Gucci's Main Man', gq.com, 2016)

p.140 Michele, Alessandro (as cited by Vogue Italia in 'Alessandro Michele: quotations, the past and future of fashion. Here's my vision.', vogue.it, 2017)

p.160 Ford, Tom (as cited by Elle UK in 'Tom Ford in conversation', elle.com, 2014)

p.172 Giannini, Frida (as cited by Sarah Y. Wu in 'Gucci Debuts Makeup Line At Milan Fashion Week Spring '15', forbes.com, 2014)

Acknowledgements

Thanks as always to my team at Ebury – Lucie, Ru and Emily, I love your work and so appreciate your encouragement and support on this series.

I have learnt everything I know from the inspirational roster of women I work with at *The Times*, namely Harriet, Anna and Hannah on the fashion desk and my all-seeing, all-brilliant editor Nicola Jeal.

I owe a big debt, as ever, to my contributors. Heartleigh, George, Julia and James, thank you for your expertise in the areas I lacked.

To my mum and dad – thank you, always.

And to my husband G, who feigned interest fantastically in his forced trip to the Gucci COSMOS exhibition when researching this book, and is always the first eye on my manuscripts, what can I say? In my book, you'll never go out of style.

About the Author

Hannah Rogers is *The Times*'s assistant fashion editor and stylist and covers whatever is contributing to the zeitgeist, specialising in trends, fashion, red carpet and celebrity. She studied anthropology and sociology at Durham University, followed by an MA in fashion journalism at Central Saint Martins, and has worked in broadsheet journalism for seven years as a writer and stylist.

Picture Credits

Images kindly provided by: Getty (p.12 Marka; p.14 Laurent Maous; p.17 Laurent Maous; p.18 WWD; p. 20 Edward Berthelot; p.24 Tiziana Fabi (left); p.24 Pietro D'Aprano (right); p.25 Christian Vierig (left); p.25 Vittorio Zunino Celotto (right); p.28 Jeremy Moeller; p.33 Streetstyleshooters; p.34 Christian Vierig; p.37 Edward Berthelot; p.37 Streetstyleshooters; p.38 Jeremy Moeller; p.41 Christian Vierig (top left); p.41 Jeremy Moeller (top right); p.41 Christian Vierig (bottom left); p.41 Streetstyleshooters (bottom right); p.42 Jeremy Moeller; p.44 Paolo Cocco; p.51 Erin Combs; p.53 Getty Images; p.56 WWD; p.59 Ron Galella, Ltd.; p.60 Edward Berthelot; p.61 Rachpoot/Bauer-Griffin (left); p.61 Edward Berthelot (right); p.62 Kevin. Mazur; p.64 Axelle/Bauer-Griffin; p.65 Jeremy Moeller; p.66 Ian Gavan; p.71 Fairchild Archive; p.73 Charley Gallay; p.75 Christian Vierig; p.76 Edward Berthelot; p.78 Edward Berthelot; p.80 Streetstyleshooters; p.81 Daniele Venturelli; p.82 Streetstyleshooters; p.83 Christian Vierig (left); p.84 Theo Wargo; p.89 Dimitrios Kambouris; p.91 Kevin Mazur; p.92 Vittorio Zunino Celotto; p.95 Gareth Cattermole; p.97 Theo Wargo; p.99 Vanni Bassetti; p.100 Kevin Mazur; p.101 Bertrand Langlois; p.102 Taylor Hill; p.104 Edward Berthelot; p.109 Christian Vierig; p.110 Edward Berthelot; p.112 Edward Berthelot (top); p.112 Edward Berthelot (bottom); p.113 Streetstyleshooters (top); p.113 Christian Vierig (bottom); p.115 Matthew Sperzel; p.117 Edward Berthelot (top left); p.117 Streetstyleshooters (top right); p.117 Christian Vierig (bottom left); p.117 Edward Berthelot (bottom right); p.118 Claudio Lavenia; p.120 Edward Berthelot; p.122 Christian Vierig; p.127 Daniele Venturelli; p.128 Jeremy Moeller; p.130 Christian Vierig; p.131 Edward Berthelot; p.133 Edward Berthelot; p.134 Edward Berthelot; p.136 Christian Vierig; p.137 Edward Berthelot; p.143 Fairchild Archive; p.144 Edward Berthelot; p.147 Edward Berthelot; p.148 Edward Berthelot; p.154 Neil Mockford; p.158 Daniele Venturelli; p.163 Emma McIntyre; p.165 Pierre Suu; p.166 Shannon Finney (left); p.166 Daniele Venturelli (right); p.168 Streetstyleshooters; p.170 Steve Granitz; p.176 Christian Vierig; p.181 Edward Berthelot; p.182 Daniele Venturelli; p.185 Edward Berthelot); Shutterstock (p.151 Brendan Beirne/Shutterstock); Unsplash (p.8 Jonas Allert; p.48 Julien Tondu; p.83 Eric Gonzalez (right); p.138 Korie Cull; p.152 James Ree; p.174 Anna Keibalo)

1

Ebury Press an imprint of Ebury Publishing,
20 Vauxhall Bridge Road,
London SW1V 2SA

Ebury Press is part of the Penguin Random House group of companies,
whose addresses can be found at global.penguinrandomhouse.com

Penguin
Random House
UK

Text by Hannah Rogers © Penguin Random House 2024
Design by maru studio G.K.

First published by Ebury Press in 2024

www.penguin.co.uk

A CIP catalogue record for this book is available from the British Library

ISBN 9781529930573

Colour origination by Altaimage Ltd, London
Printed and bound in Malaysia by Times Offset (M) Sdn Bhd

The authorised representative in the EEA is Penguin Random House Ireland,
Morrison Chambers, 32 Nassau Street, Dublin D02 YH68

Penguin Random House is committed to a sustainable future for
our business, our readers and our planet. This book is made from
Forest Stewardship Council® certified paper.